CREATIVITY

WILL SAVE THE WORLD

CREATIVITY
WILL SAVE THE WORLD
TOWARD A SPIRITUAL HUMANISM

Nicholas Berdyaev
Tom Willett (Editor)
Fr. Stephen S. Janos and
Donald A. Lowrie (Translators)

Principal matter, Nicholas Berdyaev.

Cover image: The Last Judgment,
Wassily Kandinsky

ISBN 978-0-578-87921-5

www.willett.world/creativity
creativity@willett.world

Also by Tom Willett

Nicholas Berdyaev Resource Center
www.nicholasberdyaevresourcecenter.com

Van Gogh to Go, Vol. 1
Excerpts from the Letters of
Vincent van Gogh on Art

Van Gogh to Go, Vol. 2
Excerpts from the Letters of
Vincent van Gogh on Work

Van Gogh to Go, Vol. 3
Excerpts from the Letters of
Vincent van Gogh on Spirituality

Into the Mystic
https://www.intothemysticnow.com/

willett.world
https://www.willett.world/

Contents

Editor's Introduction

As a musician and entertainment industry entrepreneur, I have long sensed that there are hidden parallels between creativity and spirituality. A true child of the '60s, I searched for signs of life through the music of Garage Rock, the British Invasion, Psychedelia, Metal and Folk, only to find myself further propelled by the combustible fusion created by adding World Music, Jazz, Classical, Experimental, Ambient, Alternative and Spoken Word to my listening habits and creative output.

After forty years of making and marketing contemporary music, I felt compelled to attempt to fashion, for lack of a better term, a "Rock and Roll Theological Aesthetic." By that I do not mean a philosophy of religious art *per se*, but an exploration into how great art, even popular music, by its sheer originality and excellence, can transport the listener from the here-and-now to what seems another realm, another place, another way of being. To quote The Door's Jim Morrison, I marvel at how compelling expressions of creativity can help us "break on through to the other side." To that I would add the wisdom of Mssrs. Jagger and Richards, "I know it's only Rock and Roll, but I like it."

Those who may have come across my work in the music business will be forgiven for wondering what a punk-ass rocker like myself is doing dabbling in philosophy. (I've taken to referring to myself as a "third-rate intellectual" to save my critics the trouble.) Even stranger may be that I have chosen an early 20th century Russian philosopher, Nicholas Berdyaev, as my patron saint. But what self-respecting Rock and Roller would not be attracted to a goateed, beret-wearing, cigar-chomping autodidact with a history of not only being kicked out of school, but twice being banished from his home country for his radical ideas about freedom, creativity and what it means to be human. Berdyaev's seminal book, *The Meaning of the Creative Act,* initially published in Russian in 1914 and first translated into English in 1955 by Donald A. Lowrie, had more effect on my understanding of the centrality of creativity to our personal and professional lives than anything else I had encountered. It brought into critical and imminent focus the perennial questions of "what does it mean to be human," "what does it mean to be an artist," and "what does it mean to be a believer in the God enfleshed in the human person of Jesus."

Prior to this season of my life, my only exposure to Russians had been through Boris and Natasha Badenov, the no-good-nik spies on the "Rocky & Bullwinkle Television Show" and Colonel Rosa Klebb, she of the lethal knife-wielding shoes in the James Bond feature film, *From Russia with Love.* The mid-life desire to balance my commercialized and hyper-kinetic life with a more contemplative approach sent me on a wandering journey through the woods of Thoreau, to the cities of St. Augustine, to the mountain of Thomas Merton, to a pilgrimage with Annie Dillard at Tinker Creek, to the impassioned letters of Vincent van Gogh, to the profane confessions and holy revelations of Henry Miller and Anaïs Nin, to the dis- and re-orienting visions of the Dada painters and poets, to a lonely, luminous walk with the French intellectual and activist, Simone Weil, and on to the provocative and liberating work of Nicholas Berdyaev.

I must confess that it's a new experience for me to traffic in overtly religious concepts and terminologies. Heretofore, my most valued insights into life have come from what a theologian would call "general revelation," the insights and epiphanies generally available to the open-hearted traveler who simply pays attention as they walk around. But Berdyaev's book is patently religious, of the Christian and Eastern Orthodox kind, and is underpinned with ideas found in theology, ontology, cosmology, anthropology, eschatology, mysticism and the apocalyptic, many with which I was not initially familiar. To those who have a similar experience while perusing this book, my heartfelt empathy and apologies. But I find his thought so compelling that even the most profane amongst us must be willing to endure a little theology in order to get to his powerful reimagining of what it means to be a human. My hope is that these invasions of the philosophical and theological are worth the slog in order to venture into the depths and heights of Berdyaev's vivifying message.

To read the dozens of books and hundreds of articles penned by Berdyaev would require an investment of time and intellectual fortitude that most of us cannot afford. Luckily, Berdyaev, himself, reported that *The Meaning of the Creative Act* contains in raw form "all my dominant and formative ideas and insights." In an effort to make this vital work all the more accessible, this thin volume presents some of the most evocative sections of *The Meaning...* as well as excerpts from other books and articles in which he further elucidates his main themes.

Some will surely find statements herein with which they feel compelled to object. Please accept my assurance that this volume is not primarily intellectual, sociological or theological in nature—nor is it propositional or argumentative in intent—but an invitation to join a world-wide salon of artists, thinkers, believers and doubters who feel compelled to further investigate the strange longing they feel for a richer life, another world, another way to be human.

A note about pronouns.... Berdyaev lived and wrote in the first half of the 20th century, a time when the use of masculine pronouns was viewed neither as discriminatory nor misogynistic. To avoid the unnecessary clanging of alarum bells, I've tried to consistently make the now-typical editorial adjustments of pronouns for the non-partisan contemporary reader.

Lastly, if my title sounds vaguely familiar, that's because it was Dostoevsky who, in his novel, *The Idiot*, first pronounced that "beauty will save the world." But that axiom seems to imply that beauty is a passive essence that just "is." Acknowledging that the experience of beauty requires both an observer and a maker, and with a trust in Fyodor's kind forbearance, I have taken the liberty to title this book, "Creativity Will Save the World."

Tom Willett
Montmartre on the Harpeth

Nicholas Berdyaev: A Biography

Nicholas Alexandrovich Berdyaev was a Russian religious philosopher who changed the philosophical and Christian landscape of the 20th century. For the Russian church, as well as for the Christian world as a whole, he was a prophet who spoke in a new way about God, humans, the Church, the meaning of history, ethics, and especially about the problems of creativity, freedom and evil. In a century when man was debased right and left, Berdyaev thought and spoke about man's dignity and purpose.

Nicholas Berdyaev was born in 1874 in the Kiev region of Ukraine into an aristocratic family. While yet still a boy, he read voraciously in his father's library, studying Hegel, Schopenhauer and Kant when he was only 14. Increasingly aware of his calling in life, he reported that "Love of philosophy and the desire to know the meaning of life pushed everything else to the margins." In the sixth form, Berdyaev left military school and was accepted to university, where Fyodor Dostoevsky, Leo Tolstoy, Henrik Ibsen, and the philosophers Søren Kierkegaard and Jakob Böhme had significant impact on his thought.

Berdyaev became a well-known figure among the thinkers of the Russian religious revival of the early 20th century. In 1919, he founded the Free Academy of Spiritual Culture in Moscow. In his book, *Self-Knowledge: An Essay in Autobiography* (also known as *Dream and Reality)*, he noted that "the significance of the Free Academy of Spiritual Culture was that during these difficult years (of civil war, Bolshevik terror, hunger and destruction) the Free Academy was, it seems, the only place where thought flowed freely and questions were posed from the qualitative heights, in terms of culture." Lecturing in the most diverse of locations, from universities to public halls to pubs, Berdyaev noted the extreme religious thirst that had taken hold of the Russian people at that time. In 1922, along with other elite representatives of Russian culture, science and theology, Berdyaev was exiled from Russia by the Soviet authorities on the renown "Philosophers' Ship." Until the end of his life he was an expatriate who dreamed of returning to his homeland.

After living in Berlin, Berdyaev moved to Paris in 1924, where he remained until his death in 1948. There, he was an active participant in the work of the Russian Christian student movement, and was friends with the leading artists and intellectuals of the Russian emigration, including Mother Maria Skobtsova, who put many of his ideas into practice. While in France he wrote 15 books and published scores of articles, and from 1925 until 1940, he was the Editor-in-Chief of the Russian journal of religious thought, *Put (The Way)*, and actively participated in the development of European philosophical life. His voluminous output was translated into dozens of languages, and he was nominated for the Nobel Prize in Literature no less than seven times.

Paul Tillich called Berdyaev "one of the most outstanding representatives of modern religious thought." His philosophy had an impact on such prominent Western thinkers as Martin Buber, Wolfhart Pannenberg, Fr. Juan Luis Segundo, Charles Hartshorne, and Jürgen Moltmann. The influence of Berdyaev's ideas affected entire theological schools, including liberation theology and process theology.

Berdyaev's main philosophical themes were God and man, freedom and creativity, and triumph over evil. He saw the Church as a Divine-human unity, in which strife and discord—the integral character of the fallen world—is overcome, and real, rather than symbolic, "unification of souls" is achieved. The Church, in which God's purpose in creation might, for the first time, be realized and fulfilled, is built on the person of the God-man, Christ, in Whom the enmity between God and man is overcome.

Berdyaev wrote that "many people believe that Christianity is primarily a religion of personal salvation when, in fact, such an interpretation is at odds with the idea of the Church, itself. Man's creativity, knowledge, art, invention, the perfection of civil society, etc. are not necessary for personal salvation, but they are necessary for the realization of God's purpose for the world and for human beings, for the transfiguration of the cosmos, for the Kingdom of God, into which the fullness of being is included. Man is called to be a creator, a co-creator in God's business of creating and managing the world, and not only 'to be saved.'"

Berdyaev died on the 23rd of March, 1948, while sitting at his desk.

Towards the end of his life, Berdyaev, whose articles and books were widely-read in Europe but not well-known in Russia, arranged for his sister-in-law, Evgenia Rapp, to transfer his archive to the USSR upon his death. Realizing the possible negative prospects for his legacy in a country where his works were banned and he, himself, had been declared a "class enemy," Berdyaev believed that if what he wrote was destined to perish, then he wanted to share the fate of his people.

Софья Андросенко (Sofia Androsenko)
Berdyaev scholar, Moscow

The Philosophic World-Outlook of Nicholas Berdyaev

N.B. Excerpts from Berdyaev's article first published in 1937 in German in Philosophen Lexicon, *"Die Philosophische Weltschaung N. A. Berdiaef." Translation © 2000 by Fr. Stephen S. Janos*

Topics: existential philosophy; anthropology; creativity; revelation; religion and culture

On Philosophy

At the center of my philosophic creativity is situated the problem of what it means to be human. And therefore my philosophy is to an utmost extent anthropologic. To posit the problem of humanity—this means at the same time to posit the problem of freedom, of creativity, person, spirit and history. Therefore, I have chiefly concerned myself with the philosophy of religion, the philosophy of history, social philosophy and ethics.

My philosophy is of the existential type, if contemporary terminology be used. But it can be likewise regarded as a philosophy of spirit. In its basic tendency this philosophy is dualistic, although the term is about dualism of a particular sort and to some measure is not ultimate. This is a dualism of spirit and nature, of freedom and determinism, of the person and the in-general, of the Kingdom of God and the kingdom of Caesar.

> ***At the center of my philosophic creativity is situated the problem of what it means to be human. And therefore my philosophy is to an utmost extent anthropologic.***

Philosophy is the discipline or science—*scientia*—concerning the soul. The *scientia* concerning the soul is however the *scientia* concerning human existence. Particularly within our existence is revealed the meaning of being. Being reveals itself through the subject, and not through the object. Philosophy therefore of necessity is anthropologic and anthropocentric.

Existential philosophy is a cognition of the meaning of being through the subject. The subject is existential—existentialized. In the object, on the contrary, the inner existence is concealed. In this sense philosophy is subjective, and not objective. It is based upon spiritual experience.

The fundamental problem of philosophy is the problem of humanity. Being reveals itself within humans and through them. We are a microcosm and a microtheos. We are created in the image and likeness of God. But at the same time we are natural beings, and finite. In humanness there is a twofold aspect: we are the point of intersection of the two worlds—we reflect in ourselves the higher world and the world lower.

As the image and likeness of God, we are persons. The person is properly distinct from the *individuum.* Person is a category which is spiritually-religious; the *individuum* however is a category which is naturalistic-biological. Person cannot be a part of anything: it is an integral whole, it is correlative to society, to nature and to God. We are spiritual beings, but also physical and fleshly. In the capacity of a fleshly being we are connected with all the cycles of worldly life, and as a spiritual being we are connected with the spiritual world and with God. The spiritual basis within persons is dependent neither upon nature nor upon society, and it is not defined by them.

On Creativity

The problem of creativity occupies a central place in my world-outlook. We were created for this: that we each in our own turn should become a creator. We are called to creative work in the world; we continue the creation of the world. The meaning and purpose of life is not accounted for merely as salvation.

> *The problem of creativity occupies a central place in my world-outlook. We were created for this: that we*

> ***each in our own turn should become a creator.***

Creativity is always a passing over from non-being to being, *i.e.* a creation from out of nothing. Creativity from nothing is a creativity from freedom. In distinction to God, however, we need material in order to create, and in our creativity there is enclosed an element issuing forth from the freedom of humanness. In the fount of our creativity there is a soaring upwards, a victory over the heaviness of the world. But in the results, in the products of creativity, there is discovered a downwards tugging and pull. In place of new being we create books, articles, pictures, social institutes, machines, cultural values. The tragedy of creativity consists in the non-correspondence of the creative intended design with its realization.

Creativity presents itself as the complete opposite of evolution. Evolution is determinism, a matter of sequential effects. Creativity however is freedom, a primordial act. The world has not ceased to be created, it is not finished—the Creation is continuing.

On Revelation

Revelation is twofold. It presupposes God, from Whom issues forth the revelation, and humans in receiving it. The acceptance of revelation is active and dependent upon the breadth or narrowness of consciousness. The world of things invisible is not forcefully compelling for us—it reveals itself in freedom. We are not free in our denial of the sensory world, which surrounds us, but we are free in our denial of God. With this is connected the mystery of faith.

> *Revelation is twofold. It presupposes God, from Whom issues forth the revelation, and humans in receiving it.*

Revelation does not contain within itself any particular philosophy, any particular system of thought. Revelation however has to be assimilated by human thought, which is made distinct by a constant activity. Theology is dependent always upon philosophic categories. But revelation cannot of necessity be bound up with any one philosophy. The capacity for changes, and the creative activity of the subject receiving the revelation, justify an eternal modernism.

On Religion

Religion is the connection between God and mankind. God is born within people, and human beings are born within God. God awaits from us a creative and free answering. With this is connected the mystery of God-humanity, of unity within duality. Christian philosophy is a philosophy of God-humanness and Christology.

> *Religion is the connection between God and mankind. God is born within people, and human beings are born within God. God awaits from us a creative and free answering. With this is connected the mystery of God-humanity, of unity within duality.*

Religious life, the primal source of which is manifest by revelation, undergoes the influences and actions of the social surroundings. This bestows on the religious history of mankind an especial complexity. There is therefore necessary a reworking of it by a constant cleansing, working it through and the reviving of it.

On Culture

Culture is the creative activity of mankind. In culture, our creativity finds its own objectivization. In theocratic societies, based on sacralization, the creative powers of people are not sufficiently free. Humanism is a liberation of the creative person and in this is comprised its truth.

Beyond the theme of culture lies concealed the theme of the relationship of people to God and to the world. Humanism in its development led to a secularization of culture, and in this secularization there was its own truth and unmasking of lie. It however finished up with a self-deification of mortal humans, and with a denial of God. And therein the image of mankind, which is in the image of God, began to disintegrate. Humanism passed over into anti-humanism. We see this with Marx and with Nietzsche.

> *Culture is the creative activity of mankind. Humanism is a liberation of the creative person and in this is comprised its truth. But humanism passed over into anti-humanism.*

The crisis of humanism presents itself as a movement towards principles supra-human, either towards Christ, or towards the Anti-Christ.

The force of technology is one of the moments of the crisis of humanism. The incursion of the masses modifies culture from above downwards, lowers its quality and leads to a crisis of spirituality. Technical civilization rends the integral wholeness of the human being and transforms us into a function. Only a spiritual renaissance would allow us to subordinate the machine to ourselves.

Berdyaev's Philosophic World-Outlook

Nicholas Berdyaev
First published in 1937 in German in *Philosophen Lexicon,* "Die Philosophische Weltschaung N. A. Berdiaef." Translation

Toward the Construction of a Christian Anthropology

N.B. Excerpts from Berdyaev's article in the journal Put, *March/April 1936, No. 50, p. 3-26 "Problema Cheloveka (K Postroeniiu Khristianskoi Antropologii)." Translation © 2000 by Fr. Stephen S. Janos*

Topics: the humanness of God; mankind as a microcosm and a microtheos; transcendence; the meaning of persons; vocation; ascesis; death as an egress from time; the mystery of creativity

There are two ways of viewing humans—from above and from below; from God and the spiritual world or from the unconscious cosmic and tellurgic forces lodged within us. I propose to examine the problem of persons as a philosopher, and not as a theologian.

This problem has become particularly urgent and tortuous for us because we sense and we feel in the experience of life and thought the insufficiency and lack of completeness of the historic approaches to anthropology, that is, patristic and scholastic anthropology, and likewise of the humanistic anthropology issuing forth from the epoch of the Renaissance. The Renaissance Christian humanism surmounted the limitations of patristic-scholastic anthropology. In any case, it was closer to the truth than was the anthropology of Luther and Calvin, negating and denying the truth about the good in mankind.

At the basis of our self-consciousness there were always two contrary senses—the sense of suppression and oppression, and that of the rising up against this suppression—the sense of exaltation and power, the capacity to create. On the one hand, we are sinful and having need for the redemption of our sin; beings basely fallen, from which is demanded humility. But on the other hand, we are created by God in accord with our Maker's image and likeness. God became human, and by this raised up our nature, and we are called into a cooperation with God and to Eternal life in God.

Human beings are a great marvel, "the connection of earth and Heaven," says Pico della Mirandola. We belong to the natural world—to the extent of being physical-chemical processes—and we are dependent upon the lower stages of nature. But in us there is an element going beyond the natural world. Greek philosophy saw this element in the reason. Aristotle proposed a definition of homo sapiens as a rational animal. Scholasticism adopted this definition. Enlightenment philosophy drew from this its own conclusions and vulgarized it.

> *We are created by God in accord with our Maker's image and likeness. God became human, and by this raised up our nature, and we are called into a cooperation with God and to Eternal life in God.*

But the self-consciousness of mankind has always been a surmounting of naturalism—it is always a self-consciousness of spirit. We are conscious of ourselves not only as natural beings but also as spiritual beings. There is in humankind a Promethean principle, and it is a sign of our God-likeness. It is not demonic, as some tend to think. But this self-consciousness is twofold: we are conscious of ourselves as both high and low, as both free and as the slave of necessity, belonging both to Eternity and situated within the power of the death-bearing stream of time.

You and I can be perceived as objects—as objects in a world of objects—and then we can be investigated by the anthropological sciences—by biology, sociology, psychology. Under such an approach it is possible to investigate only this or some other side of us; but the integrally whole person, in our depth and in our inner existence, remains elusive.

There is another approach. Each of us is conscious of ourselves foremost of all as a subject. The mysteries about mankind are revealed within the subject, within the inner existence. In objectivization, in the hurling of persons out into the objective world, the mystery is obscured and we realize about ourselves only this: that we are alienated from our inner existence.

We do not belong wholly to the objective world. We, as integral beings, do not belong to the natural hierarchy and cannot be constituted within it. Being, as subject, is act. We are a striving. In the subject is revealed the inwardly transpiring creative activity of the person.

Philosophy is anthropocentric, but we ourselves are not anthropocentric. This is a basic truth of existential philosophy.

I define existential philosophy as the opposite to a philosophy of objectification. Within the existential subject is revealed the mystery of being. Only within human existence and through our existence is there possible the cognition of being. The cognition of being is impossible through the object—through the general concepts ascribed to objects.

This consciousness (of being) is the greatest conquest of philosophy. Greek philosophy taught that being is correlative to the laws of reason. But this is only a partial truth.... There is a truth more profound. Being corresponds to an integral humanness. Being is humanized, God is humanized. Without a correspondence to the human, the cognition of the very depths of being would be impossible.

Existential philosophy, which is based upon the humanistic theory of cognition, ought to be deepened to the extent of being a theory of cognition of the Theandric—the God-human.
The human-formliness of being, and God, is from below an evident truth. From above, it reveals itself as the creation by God of mankind in God's own image and likeness.

We are a microcosm and a microtheos. God is a microanthropos. The humanness of God is a specific revelation of Christianity, setting it apart from all other religions. It is the obverse side of the Divineness or God-formliness of humans. On either side of this is, however, the God-human truth.

> ***The humanness of God is a specific revelation of Christianity, setting it apart from all other religions. It is the obverse side of the Divineness or God-formliness of humans.***

The problem of what it means to be a person can be integrally posited and resolved only in light of the idea of God-humanity. Naturalistic pondering has readily tended either towards monism, in which the one nature swallowed up the other, or towards dualism, under which God and people were completely cut off and separated by an abyss. Humanist anthropology, in acknowledging us as self-sufficient beings, was a naturalist reaction against the stifling of mankind in the traditional Christian consciousness.

We were debased as sinful beings, and

this has often produced an impression that we in general are degraded beings. Not only from our sinfulness, but from the very fact of our creatureliness, they deduced that our self-consciousness should be suppressed and debased. And from this, that we were created by God and do not possess in ourselves our own foundation, they made the inference not about the greatness of the creature, but about its nothingness.

In the dominant forms of the Christian consciousness of human beings there was acknowledged exclusively a being to be saved, and not a creative being. But the Christian anthropology always taught that we are created in the image and likeness of God. From the Eastern Teachers of the Church, St. Gregory of Nyssa did the most with anthropology, and he understands persons first of all as in the image and likeness of God. This idea was quite less developed in the West. There was the anthropology of Augustine, and from this anthropology primarily and simultaneously was defined both the Catholic and the Protestant understanding. Almost exclusively this was an anthropology of sin and the saving by grace. From the teaching about the image of God in us there was never made the ultimate conclusions. But the God-humanness of Christ bears with it the truth about the God-humanness of the each person.

> ***From the teaching about the image of God in us there was never made the ultimate conclusions. But the God-humanness of Christ bears with it the truth about the God-humanness of the each person.***

We are beings capable of rising up above ourselves, and this transcending of ourselves, this going out beyond the encircling limitations of our own selves, is a creative act. In creativity, especially, we surmount ourselves. Creativity is not a self-affirmation, but rather a self-overcoming; it is ecstatic. The very least act of men and women is creative and in it is created something not formerly existing in the world. Every live and warm relationship of person to person is the creativity of new life. Every act of love is a creative act. And it is particularly in creativity that we are in the greatest likeness to the Creator.

The creative act is always the dominion of spirit over nature and over soul, and it presupposes freedom.

First of all, it would be completely correct to say that this sick, sinful, divided being is incapable not only of creativity, but also of salvation. The possibility of salvation is grounded in the grace sent to us. But for creativity also grace is sent to us—it is given to us as gifts, genius and talent, and we hearken herein to the inner calling of God.

> *The very least act of men and women is creative and in it is created something not formerly existing in the world. Every live and warm relationship of person to person is the creativity of new life. Every act of love is a creative act. And it is particularly in creativity that we are in the greatest likeness to the Creator.*

In the creative act we go out beyond ourselves, we cease to be absorbed by ourselves and to rend at ourselves.

We cannot define ourselves only in relation to the world and other people. We ought to define ourselves, first of all, in relation to the source of our excelling, in the relationship to God.

The capacity to raise ourselves up over the natural world and over ourselves, to be a creator, depends upon facts more deep than the our faith in God, than our acknowledgement of God. It is dependent upon the *existence* of God.

The fundamental problem of anthropology is the problem of person. Person is of the category of spirit, and not nature; it is not subordinate either to nature or to society. On the contrary, society is part of the person, merely its social side. Person is likewise not part of the world, of the cosmos. Person is a microcosm. Person is a whole, it cannot be a part. The person as whole is not subordinated to any other whole, it is outside the relationships of genus and individual. Person ought to be thought of not as subordination to the genus, but in a correlation and community with other persons, with the world, and with God.

For existential philosophy, the human person has its own unique extra-natural existence, though in it there is a natural makeup. Person is contrary to thing, contrary to the world of objects. It is an active subject, an existential center. It possesses an axiological, a valuative character.

To become person is the task of each of us. To define someone as a person is a positive evaluation of them. The person is not begotten of one's parents, as is the *individuum*; it is created by God and creates itself and it is God's idea about every person. Person is a unity of destiny. This is its basic definition.

> *The fundamental problem of anthropology is the problem of person. Person is of the category of spirit, and not nature; it is not subordinate either to nature or to society.*

Together with this, person is unity in multiplicity. It cannot be comprised of parts. It has a complexly manifold makeup, but the whole in it comes before its parts. Our entire spirit-soul-bodily composition presents itself as a unique subject.

Person can contain within itself a universal content, and only person possesses this capacity. Nothing objective can contain universal content, for it is always partialized. Person accommodates within itself not the general, but the universal, the supra-personal.

The general, the abstracted idea always denotes an intellectual culture of the idol and idolatry, of making person its own tool-implement and means. Such things as statism, nationalism, scientism, communism, *etc.,* are always a transforming of person into a means and a tool. But this is never done by God. For God, the person is an end, and not a means.

Person can be conceived of only as act.

It always signifies a creative resistance. Act always is creative act. Person is creativity. Genuine activity, defining the person, is activity of spirit.

Person is resistance, resistance to the determinism of society and nature, an heroic struggle for self-definition from within. Person possesses a volitional core, in which every stirring is defined from within, and not from without.

> *Person can be conceived of only as act. It always signifies a creative resistance. Act always is creative act. Person is creativity. Genuine activity, defining the person, is activity of spirit.*

Person is pain. The heroic struggle for the realization of person is painful. It is possible to flee pain, in having forsaken to be a person. And we too often do this. To be a person, to be free, is not easy; it is difficult, a burden which we ought to bear.

Person is not something completed—it has to realize itself. This is the great task put to us, the task to realize the image and likeness of God; to accommodate within oneself in the individual form the universal, the plenitude.

Person is not self-sufficient, it cannot be satisfied with itself. It always presupposes the existence of other persons, the emergence from oneself to the other. Therein exists the opposition between person and egocentrism. Egocentrism, the immersion in one's own "I" and the beholding of everything exclusively from the point of view of this "I," the referring of everything to it, destroys the person. The realization of person presupposes the seeing of other persons. Egocentrism however shatters the function of reality in each of us.

Person presupposes diversity, the setting of a variety of persons, *i.e.* seeing realities in their true light. Solipsism, the affirming that nothing exists besides my "I" and that everything only is my "I," is a denial of person.

> *Person is not something completed——it has to realize itself. This is the great task put to us, the task to realize the image and likeness of God; to accommodate within oneself in the individual form the universal, the plenitude.*

Person presupposes sacrifice, but it is impossible to sacrifice the person. It is possible to sacrifice one's life, and one sometimes ought to sacrifice his life, but no one has the right to renounce his own person. Everyone ought to in sacrifice and through sacrifice remain to the end a person. To renounce one's own person is impossible, since this would signify a renouncing of God's idea about us, in effect the non-realizing of God's intent.

It is not necessary for person to be renounced, but rather there should be renounced the hardened selfness in stirring the person to unfold itself. In the creative act, which is the realization of person, there ought to occur a sacrificial pouring off of selfness, in defining us from other people, from the world and from God.

We are beings in ourselves insufficient, dissatisfied, but surmounting ourselves by our lives in the most remarkable acts. Person is forged out in this creative self-definition. It always presupposes the vocation, the singular and unrepeated calling of each one. It follows an inner voice, calling it to realize its own task in life. We only then are persons when we follow this inner voice, rather than external influences. Vocation always bears an individual character. And no one other can decide the question about the vocation of a given person. We possess a vocation in that we are called to creativity. Creativity, however, is always an individual matter.

The realization of person presupposes *ascesis*. But it is impossible to conceive of *ascesis* as an end, as something hostile to the world and to life. *Ascesis* is but a means, a drilled work-out, a concentration of inner powers. Person presupposes *ascesis* in that it is an intensifying and a resistance, a non-accord to be defined by nature or society. The attainment of an inner self-definition demands *ascesis.*

But *ascesis* easily degenerates—it becomes transformed into an end-in-itself, so as to embitter the heart, and make us ill-disposed towards life. And then it becomes hostile towards us and the person.

The need for *ascesis* is not in denying our creativity, but to realize this creativity.

> ***Vocation always bears an individual character. And no one other can decide the question about the vocation of a given person. We possess a vocation in that we are called to creativity. Creativity, however, is always an individual matter.***

Person is diverse yet unified; unrepeatable, original, not the same as others. Person is the exception, and not the rule.

We stand afront a paradoxical combination of opposites: of the personal and the supra-personal, of the finite and the Infinite, of the unchanging and the changing, of freedom and of fate. Ultimately, there is a fundamental antinomy connected with the person.

The creative act realizes the new, something not formerly in the world. But it presupposes the creative subject, in which is given the possibility of self-determination and self-uplifting within creativity of the formerly non-extant. To be a person is difficult; to be free means to take upon oneself a burden. The easiest thing of all would be to renounce the person and to renounce freedom; to live under determinism, under authority.

There is within man a subconscious elemental basis connected with cosmic life and with the earth, a cosmic-tellurgic element. The very passions connected with the natural-elemental basis would seem to be the material from which also are created the greatest virtues of the person. The intellectual-moral and rational denying of the natural-elemental within us leads to the desiccation and stoppage of the wellsprings of life. When consciousness chokes off and squeezes out the sub-conscious element, there then occurs a dividing of our nature and its petrifying and ossification.

The path of the realization of persons runs from the sub-conscious through the conscious to the supra-conscious. Consciousness must needs be thought of dynamically, and not statically; it can shrink or it can expand, it can hide away whole worlds or it can reveal them. But an egress from this median-norm consciousness is possible and with it is connected all of our utmost attainments; with it is connected sanctity and genius, contemplation and creativity. The importance and the interesting aspect in human beings is connected with this opening up in us of the path towards the Infinite and the Eternal, with the possibility of breaking through.

Wherefore, only with person is there also a paradoxical conjoining of the finite and the Infinite. Person is a going out from itself, beyond its limits, but not allowing of dissolution and being mixed away. There is therefore within the person a sub-conscious foundation, there is the conscious and there is the egress to the supra-conscious.

The body belongs inalienably to the person, the image of God in us. The spiritual principle vivifies both the soul and the body. The body can become spiritualized, can become a spiritual body, whilst not ceasing to be a body. The Eternal principle within the body is not in its physical-chemical constitution, but in its form. Without this form there is no integrally whole image of the person. Flesh and blood do not inherit life Eternal, *i.e.* the materiality of our fallen world does not inherit, but the spiritizing bodily form does inherit.

> *The importance and the interesting aspect in human beings is connected with this opening up in*

> ***us of the path towards the Infinite and the Eternal, with the possibility of breaking through.***

Our body in this sense is not only one of the objects of the natural world, it has also an existential meaning, it belongs to an inner, non-objectivized existence, it belongs to the integrative subject. The realization of the form of the body leads to the realization of person. This means precisely the liberation from the rule of body, having subordinated its spirit. We live in an epoch when we, and foremost of all our bodies, seem unsuited for the new technical means conceived of by ourselves. We are fragmented.

But person is an integral spirit-soul-body being, in which the soul and the body are subordinated to spirit, spiritized, and by this conjoined with the higher, the supra-personal and supra-human being. Suchlike is our inner hierarchy. Spirit is not a nature within us, distinct from the nature of soul and body, but rather an immanently acting within its gracious power (breath and breathing), the utmost quality of human beings. Spirit manifests itself as the genuinely acting and creative in mankind.

We cannot define ourselves only afront life. We ought also to define ourselves afront death. We ought to live, knowing that we will die. Death is a most important fact of human life, and we cannot worthily live not having defined our relationship towards death. Endless life in this world would be bereft of meaning. The positive meaning of death is in this, that the fullness of life cannot be realized in time, in not only a finite span of time, but neither in endless time. The fullness of life can be realized only in Eternity, only beyond the limits of time, because in time life remains without meaning if it has not received its meaning from Eternity.

But the egress from time to Eternity is a leap across the abyss. In the fallen world this leap across the abyss is termed death. (But) there is another egress from time into Eternity—through the depth of the moment, comprising neither a fragmented part of time nor subject to numeric quantity. But this egress is neither final nor integral, and constantly again one falls back into time.

> *But the egress from time to Eternity is a leap across the abyss. In the fallen world this leap across the abyss is termed death. There is another egress from time into Eternity——through the depth of the moment, comprising neither a fragmented part of time nor subject to numeric quantity. But this egress is neither final nor integral, and constantly again one falls back into time.*

Christianity teaches not about the immortality of the soul, but about the resurrection of the integrally whole human being, of the person; of the resurrection of the body also, as belonging to the person. Only the Christian teaching about resurrection affirms immortality as the Eternity of the integral wholeness of the person. In a certain sense it can be said that immortality is a conquest of spiritual creativity, the victory of the spiritual person, endowed with body and soul, over the natural *individuum*.

The realization of person for Eternal life has moreover a connection with the problem of sex and love. Sex is a halfness, a fragmentedness, a non-fullness of the person, an anguish of incompleteness. The integrally whole person is bi-sexualized, androgenic. The metaphysical meaning of love is in the attainment of the integral wholeness of person for life Eternal.

We can realize ourselves only in community with other persons, in communality. Community is always personalistic, it is always an encounter of person with person, the "I" with the "thou" in a "we." This poses the question about the nature of the Church in the existential meaning of the word, *i.e.* as an authentic community, of the communality or *"sobornost,"* of the "I" and the "thou" in the "we," in a Divine-human body, in the Body of Christ. The society at the foundation of which would be posited personalism, the avowal of the supreme value of every person and of the existential relationship of person to person, such a society would be transformed into communality, (into the Church).

But communality is unattainable by way of the compulsive organization of society; by this way may be created a more just order, but not the brotherhood of people. In communality, the "I" with the "thou" in the "we" imperceptibly passes over into the Kingdom of God.

Christian anthropology is embedded in the problem of a Christian sociology. But the problem of persons takes primacy over the problem of society. We are not creations of society in its image and likeness; we are a creation of God in God's image and likeness. Humans possess within themselves an element independent of society, we realize ourselves within society, but we are not wholly dependent upon it. Sociology ought to be grounded upon anthropology, and not the reverse.

The final, the ultimate problem upon which philosophic and religious anthropology devolves is the problem of the relationship of the person to history. This is an eschatological problem. History is the fated-destiny of humans. It is a tragic fate. We are not only social beings, but also historical being. We are trampled down by history. There exists a most profound conflict between history and humanity, between the ways of history and our ways. We are drawn into history, we become subject to its fate and together with this we find ourselves in conflict with it; we oppose to history the value of person, its inner life and individual destiny. Within the bounds of history this conflict is irresolvable.

> *The final, the ultimate problem upon which philosophic and religious anthropology devolves is the problem of the relationship of the human person, to history. This is an eschatological problem.*

History, in its religious meaning, is movement towards the Kingdom of

God. And this religious meaning is realized only when there is a breaching through of history by the meta-historical.

There has never been a personalist revolution, a revolution in the name of the person, of every human person, in the name of the realization of the fullness of life for it.

The philosophy of history however is inevitably eschatology. The philosophy of history is not so much a teaching about the meaning of history through progress, as rather the teaching of the meaning of history through the end. Christian anthropology ought to be posited not only in the perspective of the past, *i.e.* oriented towards Christ crucified, as up to the present has been done, but also to the perspective of the future, *i.e.* oriented towards Christ coming again, risen in power and glory. But the appearance of Christ coming is dependent upon the creative deed of each of us—it is prepared for by us. The insufficiency and defect of humanist anthropology was not at all in that it emphasized mankind too much, but rather in that it insufficiently affirmed his finality of end.

> *The appearance of Christ coming is dependent upon the creative deed of each of us——it is prepared for by us.*

Humanism had Christian sources and at the beginning of the modern period there existed a Christian humanism. But in its ultimate development, humanism assumed the forms of affirming the self-sufficiency of men and women. At the very moment when they proclaim that there is nothing higher than us, that for us there is nowhere up to go and that we are sufficient unto ourselves, we then begin to take on and be subject to the lower nature.

We can be raised up only by the awareness that we are in the image and likeness of God, *i.e.* is a spiritual being, exalted over the natural and social world and summoned to transfigure it and be master over it. The self-affirmation of mankind leads to the self-destruction of mankind. Suchlike is the fatal dialectic of humanism.

But we ought not to deny every truth of humanism, as is done by many a reactionary theological tendency, but rather to affirm a creative Christian humanism, one that is theandric, connected with the revelation about God-humanness.

In what is the meaning of creativity? This meaning is quite more profound than the usual justification of cultural and social creativity. The creative act essentially does not demand a justification, and this is an external positing of the question, for it justifies, and is not justified. The creative act, presupposing a freedom external to being, is in answer to God's call and it is needful for the Divine life, itself, wherein we possess not only an anthropogonic, but also a theogonic significance. The ultimate mystery about human beings, which we are able to comprehend only with difficulty, is connected with this—that we and our creative deeds have significance for the Divine life, itself; they represent a fulfillment for Divine life.

> *The ultimate mystery about human beings, which we are able to comprehend only with difficulty, is connected with this——that we and our creative deeds have significance for the Divine life, itself; they represent a fulfillment for Divine life.*

The mystery of creativity remains hidden and unrevealed in the Holy Scripture. In the name of our freedom, God provides us ourselves the opportunity to uncover the meaning of our creativity. Through the God-human Christ, our nature is a communicant in the Holy Trinity and in the depths of Divine life. There exists a from-all-Eternity humanness within the Trinity and it signifies also the Divine within us.

> *Through the God-human Christ, human nature is a communicant in the Holy Trinity and in the depths*

> *of Divine life. There exists a from-all-Eternity humanness within the Trinity and it signifies also the Divine within us .*

The creative act, therefore, is a self-discovery within the fullness of Divine life. The authentic creativity of men and women is Christological, though this be not evidently perceived. Humanism does not comprehend this depth of the problem of creativity; it remains at the secondary. The Christian consciousness, however, bound up with the social everyday ordinary in life, has remained closed off from the creative mystery of being; it was oriented exclusively towards the struggle with sin. And thus it has been up to the present.

But the appearance of a new self-consciousness within Christianity is possible. Anthropologic investigations ought to prepare for it from various sides. The traditional Christian anthropology, as also the traditional philosophic anthropology, both the idealistic and the naturalistic, ought to be surmounted. The teaching about humans as creators is a creative task for modern thought.

Nikolai Berdyaev
From the journal *Put*, March/April 1936, No. 50, p. 3-26, "Problema Cheloveka (K Postroeniiu Khristianskoi Antropologii)." Translation

Two Understandings of Christianity: Salvation and Creativity

N.B. Excerpts from Berdyaev's article in the journal Put, *January 1926, No. 2, p. 26-46 "Spasenie I Tvorchestvo, Dva Ponimaniya Khristianstvva." Translation © 1999 by Fr. Stephen S. Janos*

Topics: the justification of creativity; the church and the world; the sacred and the mundane

The correlation between the ways of human salvation and the ways of human creativity is very central, very tormenting, and a very acute problem of our age.

Mankind perishes and has a thirst for salvation. But we are also by our nature makers, creators, builders of life, and the thirst for creativity cannot be extinguished within us. Can we be saved and at the same time create, can we create and at the same time be saved?

And how to perceive Christianity: is Christianity exclusively the religion of the salvation of the soul for life Eternal, or is creativity of a higher life also justified by the Christian consciousness? All these questions torment the contemporary soul, though not always is perceived their depth. Wanting to set right their life vocation, their creative act of life, Christians do not always realize that there is discourse about the very concept of Christianity, about the assimilation of its fullness.

> *Wanting to set right their life vocation, their creative act of life, Christians do not always realize that there is discourse about the very concept of Christianity, about the assimilation of its fullness.*

The torment of the problem of salvation and creativity reflects the schisms betwixt Church and world, the spiritual and the mundane, the sacral and the secular. The Church is concerned with salvation; the secular world however is concerned with creativity. There is a profound disdain, almost a contempt of the churchly world towards those creative deeds in the life of culture, in the life of society, which fully are processes, transpiring within the world. The creative act, which the secular world is concerned with, is not given justification, is not sanctified by the Church. At best creativity is admitted, it is tolerated; one peeks at it through the fingers, not granting it a profound justification. (To the Church) salvation is a matter of the first sort, the one thing necessary. Creativity, however, is a matter of the second... or third sort, applicable to life, but not the very essence of it.

The religious non-expression of the human principle as an organic part of the life of God-humanness creates the dualism of Church and world, of Church and culture, the acute dualism of the sacral and the profane. For the believing Christian, two lives are created—a life that is of a first and another a second sort. And this dualism, this two-sidedness of life, attains to an especial acuteness in the Christianity of the present time. The

Christian of the present time lives in two incongruent rhythms—in the Church and in the world; upon the pathways of salvation and upon the pathways of creativity.

> *The creative act, which the secular world is concerned with, is not given justification, is not sanctified by the Church. At best creativity is admitted, it is tolerated; one peeks at it through the fingers, not granting it a profound justification.*

Six days in the week we devote to our creative, constructive work. And our creative attitude towards life remains non-justified, non-sanctified, not co-dependent upon the religious principle of life. The very believers, the selfsame people, participate in the non-justified and the non-sanctified life of the world; they subordinate themselves to the profane, the non-sacral science, to the profane non-sacral economy, to the profane non-sacral law, to a lifestyle long since already bereft of sacral character.

The believers live the church life in Church; they go on Sundays and feast days to the temple, they fast during Great Lent, they pray to God morning and evening, but they do not live church life in the world, in culture, in society. Their creativity, in political and economic life, in the sciences and the arts, in the inventions and the discoveries, in everyday morality, remains external to the Church and external to religiosity; it remains profane and worldly. This is altogether an other rhythm of life.

A tempestuous creative development has transpired within the world, in culture. In the Church, however, a comparative staticism has set in, as though petrified and ossified. The Church hierarchy became hostile towards creativity and suspicious towards spiritual culture. It restrains man and fears his freedom. The ways of salvation are put opposite the ways of creativity. We are saved on one plane of existence, and we fashion life on altogether another plane of existence. And there remains always the danger that on that plane on which we create, we shall perish and not be saved.

And how often the most reactionary tendencies of Church thought have appropriated to themselves a nominalistic understanding of the Church. They have ceased to comprehend the Church integrally, as a universal spiritual organism, as ontologic reality, as the Christified cosmos.

> *Christianity cannot be reduced to the individual salvation of separate souls. The understanding of Christianity exclusively as a religion of personal salvation would be the source of the greatest disorders and catastrophes in the Christian world.*

The Church was transformed into a curative establishment in which they deal with individual souls for healing. Thus is affirmed a Christian individualism, indifferent to the fate of society and the world. The Church exists for the salvation of individual souls, but has no concern for the creative aspects of life, for the transfiguration of social and cosmic life.

Christianity cannot be reduced to the individual salvation of separate souls. The collapse of theocracy ought to lead to the awakening of creative activism of a very Christian nation, a human activism, for the formation of a Christian society. This turnabout should begin first of all with this, that church people make themselves responsible for the fate of the Church in the world, in an historical actuality; that they be obliged to take upon themselves churchly formation, the life of the parishes, a concern about the temple, and organization of churchly life, brotherhoods, *etc.* But this change of psychology cannot be restricted to formation of churchly life; it extends also to all aspects of life. All of life ought to be thought of as churchly life.

The understanding of Christianity exclusively as a religion of personal salvation, the constriction of the scope of the Church to something existing alongside with everything else—when the Church is the posited fullness of being—would be also the source of the greatest disorders and catastrophes in the Christian world.

Nikolai Berdyaev
From the journal *Put*, January 1926, No. 2, p. 26-46 “Spasenie I Tvorchestvo, Dva Ponimaniya Khristianstvva.”

Creativity and Redemption

N.B. Excerpts from "Creativity and Redemption," The Meaning of the Creative Act, *1914, Chapter 3. Translation © 1955 by Donald A. Lowrie*

Topics: the anthropological revelation of life; the World-Epoch of Creativeness; the Christology of humans

New Testament Christianity is a religion of redemption, the good news of salvation from sin, the revelation of the Son of God, the second hypostasis of the Holy Trinity in the aspect of God suffering for the sins of the world. This is one of the stages on the spiritual road.

But does the mystery of salvation take in the whole of life? Is life's final purpose only salvation from sin? Redemption from sin, salvation from evil, are in themselves negative, and the final aims of being lie far beyond, in a positive creative purpose.

The absolute Christian truth turns on the one hand towards redemption from sin and evil, and on the other towards our positive creative calling: it reveals a Christology of mankind.

There is not one word in the Gospel about creativeness: by no amount of sophism can we derive from the Gospel creative challenges and imperatives. That the ways of creativeness are hidden in New Testament Christianity is providential.

> *Does the mystery of salvation take in the whole of life? Is life's final purpose only salvation from sin? Redemption from sin, salvation from evil, are in themselves negative, and the final aims of being lie far beyond, in a positive creative purpose.*

Mankind's creative activity has no Holy Scriptures: its ways are not revealed to us from above. In creativeness, we are, as it were, left to ourselves, alone, and have no direct aid from on high. And in this fact the great wisdom of God is evident.

> ***The absolute Christian truth turns on the one hand towards redemption from sin and evil, and on the other towards our positive creative calling: it reveals a Christology of mankind.***

We feel the holy authority of the Gospel's silence about creativeness. This absolute silence of Holy Scripture about our creative activity is Divinely wise. And to discern the all-wise meaning of this silence is to discern the mystery about us; it is an act of our highest self-consciousness.

If the ways of creativeness were indicated and justified in the Holy Scriptures, then creativeness would be obedience, which is to say that there would be no creativeness.

The revelation of creativeness does not come from above, but rather from below—it is an anthropological, not a theological, revelation. God revealed God's will to sinful persons in the Law and granted us the grace of Redemption, sending into the world His Only Son. And God awaits from us an anthropological revelation of creativity; in the name of our God-like freedom, God has hidden from us the ways of creativeness and the justification of creativeness.

Creativeness is a work of our God-like freedom, the revelation of the image of the Creator within us. Creativeness is not in the Father, neither is it in the Son, but in the Spirit. Hence it goes beyond the borders of the Old and New Testaments. Where the Spirit is, there is freedom, and there, too, is creativeness.

> *Creativeness is a work of our God-like freedom, the revelation of the image of the Creator within us. Creativeness is not in the Father, neither is it in the Son, but in the Spirit.*

Creativeness is not related to the

priesthood and does not resemble it. Creativeness is in the spirit of prophecy. The Spirit cannot have its Scriptures—it knows no directives: it is revealed in freedom. The Spirit breatheth where it will. Life in the Spirit is free and creative life. The anthropological revelation, which has its origin in Christ, is finally completed in the Spirit, in the free creative activity of us living in the Spirit.

In creativeness, the Divine in us is revealed by our own free initiative, revealed from below rather than from above. In creativeness we ourselves reveal the image and likeness of God in us, manifest the Divine power within us.

The breathing of the Spirit is not only Divine, it is Divine-human as well. The Church, too, is a Divine-human organism.

The mystery of the redemption was accomplished, and is eternally being accomplished, in the cosmos. After the redemption, a new creative being appears in the world and we are called to extraordinary activity, to creative upbuilding of profit for the Kingdom of God which is known as God-humanity.

The Creator's idea of us is sublime and beautiful. So sublime and so beautiful is the Divine idea of us that creative freedom, the free power to reveal ourselves in creative action, is placed within us as a seal and sign of our likeness to God, as a mark of the Creator's image.

> *The mystery of the redemption was accomplished, and is eternally being accomplished, in the cosmos. After the redemption, a new creative being appears in the world and we are called to extraordinary activity, to creative upbuilding of profit for the Kingdom of God which is known as God-humanity.*

The compulsory revelation of creativeness as a law, as an indication of the way to go, would contradict

God's idea of us, God's desire to see in us the creator, reflecting God's own Divine nature.

If there had been a revelation about creativeness from above, a revelation imprinted in the Holy Scriptures, then our free creative deed would have been both unnecessary and impossible. There would have remained no room for an anthropological revelation. Such a passive concept of human nature makes us beings unworthy of the incarnation. Christ would not have been God-human if our nature is merely passive, un-free, and reveals nothing from within itself. For truly the God-human is a revelation not only of Divine but of our greatness, and predicates faith not only in God, but in us, as well.

The redemption, itself, was an inner growth of we as God's creatures. In the spirit of humanness, all the mystical events of the life of Christ are accomplished.

Our likeness to God in God's only Son

is already the everlasting basis for our independent and free nature, capable of creative revelation.

God did not reveal from above that He wills free courageous action in creativeness. If God had revealed and established this in Holy Scriptures, then free courageous action would be unnecessary and impossible. The truth about free daring in creativeness may be revealed by us ourselves, alone, only in a free act of our own daring. Herein lies hidden the great mystery of persons.

And there can be no Divine revelation of this secret; it is inevitably hidden. The creative secret is both hidden from us and revealed by us. This is an esoteric mystery of Divine revelation and of Holy Scripture.

God the Creator, by an act of God's almighty and omniscient will, created us—God's own image and likeness, beings free and gifted with creative power, called to be lords of creation.

This is an inner process in God. By an act of God's almighty and omniscient power, the Godhead willed to limit their own foresight of what our creative freedom would reveal, since such foreknowledge would have done violence to and limited our freedom in creation.
The Creator does not wish to know what the anthropological revelation will be. Herein we see the great and sublime wisdom of God in the work of creation. God wisely concealed from us God's will that we should be called to be free and daring creators and concealed what we would create in this free courageous action.

By a free act of God's absolute will, God the Creator excluded from creating all violence and compulsion, having desired only the freedom and the courageous activity of the creature. God waits for our answering love: God waits for a free response to His call.

Creativeness is not only the struggle with sin and evil—it wills another world, it continues the work of creation.

The Law begins the struggle against sin and evil; the Redemption finishes that struggle; but we are called to create a new and hitherto unknown world through free and daring creativeness, to continue God's creation.

The fundamental duality of our nature, our belonging to two worlds, corresponds to the duality of redemption and creativeness. As a fallen being, enslaved by the results of sin and caught by the force of necessity, we must pass through the mystery of redemption, in it must restore our God-like nature, regain our lost freedom. The creative secret of being is hidden by sin. Mankind's creative powers are weakened by our fall.

Through Christ, our nature is redeemed and restored; we are saved from the curse of sin. The old person is reborn into a new creature, the New Adam. But the mystery of redemption conceals the mystery of creativeness. As a God-like being, belonging to the realm of freedom, we are called to reveal our creative power. Here is the other side of our dualistic nature, oriented towards creativeness instead of redemption.

But true creativeness is possible only through redemption. Christ became immanent in human nature, and this makes us a creator like the Creator God.

The world has not yet seen a religious Epoch of Creativeness. The world knows only the religious epochs of the Old Testament Law and New Testament Redemption. The world has lived in either religious obedience or sinful disobedience.

> ***The world has not yet seen a religious Epoch of Creativeness. The world only the religious epochs of the Old Testament Law and New Testament Redemption.***

We are standing on the threshold of a World-Epoch of religious Creativeness, on a cosmic divide. Up to now all the creativeness of "culture" has been only a preparatory hint, the sign of the real creativeness of another world. In the creativeness of "culture" there is expressed only the tragic dualism of our nature, struggling to escape from the fetters of necessity but not yet attaining another sphere of being. Just as bloody pagan sacrifice was merely a foreshadowing of the world's true redemption through Christ's sacrifice on Golgotha, a foreshadowing which did not attain true redemption, so our creative efforts, which have brought into being the values of culture, have been up to now only a foreshadowing of a true religious Epoch of Creativeness which will realize another sphere of being.

The religious Epoch of Creativeness will be a transition into another sphere of being, not merely to another "culture" or to another sphere of "science and art." The religious Epoch of Creativeness is a Third Revelation, an anthropological revelation following those of the Old and New Testaments.

The ancient world moved towards

redemption before the appearance of Christ. So the new world moves towards creativeness, but it has not yet known nor could it know creativeness until there is a cosmic anthropological turning-point, until there is a great religious revolution in self-consciousness. Then it will be seen that the creativeness of "culture" was a poor substitute for the creativeness of "being" in the Epoch of the Law and the Redemption, when our creative powers were still suppressed.

From this tragic problem of Christianity there can be only one way out: the religious acceptance of the truth that the religious meaning of life and being is not wholly a matter of redemption from sin, that life and being have positive, creative purposes.

That higher creative, positive being, though unattainable at the time when redemption was begun, when God was still transcendent to us, is attainable in another period of religious life, after the redemption, when God in us is immanent.

> *The religious Epoch of Creativeness is a Third Revelation, an anthropological revelation following those of the Old and New Testaments.*

Salvation from sin, from perdition, is not the final purpose of religious life: salvation is always *from* something and life should be *for* something. Many things unnecessary for salvation are needed for the very purpose for which salvation is necessary—for the creative upsurge of being. Our chief end is not to be saved, but to mount up creatively.

The third creative revelation in the Spirit will have no Holy Scripture; it will be no voice from on high; it will be accomplished in humanity—it is an anthropological revelation, an unveiling of the Christology of mankind.

God awaits the anthropological revelation from us, and we cannot expect to have it from God.

> *Salvation from sin is not the final purpose of religious life:*

> *salvation is always* from *something and life should be* for *something.*

And one cannot merely wait for the Third Revelation; we must accomplish it ourselves, living in the Spirit; accomplish it by a free, creative act. In this act everything transcendent will become immanent. We are quite free in the revelation of our creativeness. In this fearful freedom lies all of our God-like dignity, and our dread responsibility. The virtue of accepting a dangerous position, the virtue of daring to do, is the basic virtue of the Creative Epoch.

Only we who possess these virtues will vision the Coming Christ: only to us will the mighty and glorified Christ come. We who coward-like refuse the terrible burden of the final freedom cannot be oriented towards the Coming Christ—that person is not making ready Christ's Second Coming.

Only a sacrificial resolve to take a risky and dangerous place, to sail away from safe shores towards an unknown and yet undiscovered continent from which no helping hands reach out—only this terrible liberty makes man worthy to see the Absolute Man, in Whom is finally revealed the creative secret of mankind.

The Coming Christ will reveal Christ's creative mystery to we who ourselves do daring deeds of creativeness, who are preparing a New Heaven and a New Earth.

Our creativeness in the Spirit, in the higher spiritual life, is preparing for the Second Coming of Christ. The way to the Second Coming requires active courage.... We are called not merely to wait and have a presentiment, but to act and to create. We must move out of a religious-passive and receptive condition into one of religious activity and creativeness.

> *The way to the Second Coming requires active courage.... We are called not merely to wait and have a presentiment, but to act and to*

| *create.*

God gave us the gracious aid of Christ's redemption which restored our fallen nature. Through the redemption, our creative freedom is restored to us. And the time must come in the world for this creative freedom to be active. We must create that for which we were redeemed, for which we were created.

Christianity makes God immanent in our nature and hence cannot admit a completely transcendent separation between this world and the next.
The question of the religious meaning of creativeness has never before been put—such a question has never arisen in consciousness. This is the question of our time, one question, the final question to which the crisis of all culture leads us.

The religious problem of creativeness is a problem of the ways of another kind of religious experience, of building up another kind of being. Creativeness is neither permitted nor justified by religion—creativeness is itself religion.

Creative experience is a special kind of experience and a special kind of way: the creative ecstasy shatters the whole of our being—it is an out-breaking into another world.

> *The question of the religious meaning of creativeness has never before been put. This is the question of our time, one question, the final question to which the crisis of all culture leads us.*

At its best, Christianity justified creativeness, but it never rose to the consciousness that what matters is not to justify creativeness but by creativeness to justify life. Creativeness is the final revelation of the Holy Trinity—its anthropological revelation.

In the mystery of redemption the Creator's boundless love towards us and God's boundless grace were poured out. In the mystery of creativeness, our boundless nature is revealed and our highest calling is realized.

Love is not only grace, but the activity of we, ourselves, as well. God, who gave God's only Son to be broken on the tree, atones for the sin of mankind, and God expects that we, having partaken of the mystery of the redemption, will accomplish the great deed of creativeness, will realize our positive destiny.

Human nature is creative because it is the image and likeness of God the Creator. That we as creatures cannot fail to be ourselves creators is an anthropological truth which was not recognized with sufficient intensity and fullness by former religious epochs.

Religious consciousness was full of the mystery of redemption of our nature, but the mystery of this to-be-redeemed nature, itself, was unknown. What is the pre-destination of this redeemed nature? Within the limits of the religion of redemption, there is no answer to this question.

It is as though the persons who are redeemed from their sins desired that their human nature should cease to exist—that only the Divine nature alone should exist. But Christ is God-human. Christ redeems and restores our nature to its likeness unto God.

Human nature which knows itself, knows its independent and free being, must exist Eternally only as a creative and creating nature. We finally justify ourselves before the Creator not by extinguishing ourselves but by our own creative expression. We must absolutely be.

Human nature, redeemed and saved from evil, has a positive content and a positive purpose. This content and purpose is creativeness.

> *Human nature is creative because it is the image and likeness of God the Creator. That we as creatures cannot fail to be ourselves creators is an anthropological truth which was not recognized with sufficient intensity and fullness by former religious epochs.*

Our creativeness is connected with the ecstatic element in us. This element exists in a fallen and sinful state. It is cleansed and enlightened by redemption, not quenched or destroyed. The cleansed and illuminated creative ecstasy realizes our calling.

Repentance or purification is only one of the moments of religious experience, one of the acts of the mystery of Christ. We must not stop at this moment: we must go on to positive spiritual living.

God's will must be fulfilled to the uttermost; here there can be no difference of opinion among Christians. But we have to know what the will of God is. We dare not understand it in a purely formal way. And is not the fulfillment of the secret will of God our free creativity?

Nicholas Berdyaev
From "Creativity and Redemption,"
The Meaning of the Creative Act, 1914, Chapter 3. Translation © 1955 by Donald A. Lowrie

Creativity and Asceticism: The Genius and the Saint

N.B. Excerpts from "Creativity and Asceticism: The Genius and the Saint," The Meaning of the Creative Act, *1914, Chapter 7. Translation © 1955 by Donald A. Lowrie*

Topics: asceticism; creative ecstasy; genius v. talent

In the depths of every true religion and every genuine mystic there is the thirst for overcoming "the world" as a lower order of being, and hence we have asceticism as a way to this conquest and this victory. Without this ascetic moment—that is, the conquest of this world for the sake of another world—religious and mystical life is unthinkable.

But we are faced with the question: is there some other religious way? The experience of creative ecstasy as a religious way is not revealed in the consciousness of the Church Fathers or in the consciousness of the old mystics. It is either denied completely as "worldly" and of the passions, or else is merely admitted and permitted. At best, religious consciousness justifies creativeness; but this very religious justification of creativeness presupposes that creativeness lies outside the way of religion.

Creative experience is not something secondary and hence requiring justification. Creative experience is something primary, and hence justifying. Creativeness is no less spiritual, no less religious, than asceticism. Creative ecstasy is a religious ecstasy.

> ***Creativeness is no less spiritual, no less religious, than asceticism. Creative ecstasy is a religious ecstasy.***

Creativeness accepts the Gospel commandment not to love "the world" or the things of the world. He who creates feels herself to be not of this world. Creativeness is the overcoming of the world in the Gospel sense, but a kind of overcoming other than that of asceticism, although equal to it in value.

In the creative act, we pass out from this world and enter another world. Likewise, creativeness is not an adaptation to this world—creativeness is transition beyond the limits of this world.

The Gospel commandments "love not the world" and "overcome the world" remain valid forever and can never be revoked. To "not love the world" means to be free and to reveal our kinship to God.... Creativeness is not only faithful to this highest commandment of freedom from "the world," but it is also, by its very nature, a victory over that world in the name of another. It is a revelation of the meaning of the commandment "love not the world."

The creative act is always an exit from "this world," from this life. In its essence, creativeness is an unshackling, a bursting of chains. In the creative

ecstasy all the heaviness of the world is overcome; sin is burned away; an other, a higher nature, shines through.
The experience of overcoming the world in creativeness is qualitatively different from the ascetic experience of overcoming the world. It is not an experience of obedience, but rather an experience of daring. "The world" is burned away in the daring of creative activity just as in the act of obedience.

> *In the creative ecstasy all the heaviness of the world is overcome; sin is burned away; an other, a higher nature, shines through.*

Creative values are not "worldly," not "of this world." The creative act is transcendental: it steps outside "the world."

The Christian consciousness ascetically denies "the world" and everything worldly—in this is the Eternal truth. And criticism of historic Christianity is rightly directed at its compromises and "deals" with "the world." Historic

Christianity is lacking in consistent asceticism; in its expression it is not yet sufficiently spiritual.

There is neither contradiction nor opposition between creativeness and asceticism. Creativeness does not assert what asceticism denies. The revelation of creativeness lies outside the Gospel's denial of "the world." Creativeness presupposes an ascetic overcoming of the world—it is positive asceticism.

Creative life is life Eternal, and not life corruptible.

> *There is neither contradiction nor opposition between creativeness and asceticism. Creativeness does not assert what asceticism denies. The revelation of creativeness lies outside the Gospel's denial of "the world." Creativeness presupposes an ascetic overcoming of the world——it is positive asceticism.*

How powerless and pitiful is all moralizing about great creations! (Any evil that might be in an artist's nature) is consumed by passing through the creative ecstasy of genius. The beauty which is born in the creative act is a transition from "this world" into the cosmos, into another form of being, and in it there can be no shadow of the evil which was in the sinful nature of the creator.

The spiritual life is unthinkable without the great mystery of repentance. Sin must be not only recognized but it must be consumed in the fire of repentance. Creativity cannot replace repentance. The creative ecstasy and the creative impulse are a revolutionary birth into new life.

In the religious creative experience there is a positive rather than a negative overcoming of "the world." The world must be conquered both ascetically and creatively. But by the ascetic way alone, solely by repentance, "the world" cannot be overcome, sin and darkness cannot be finally burned away.

In Christian saintliness there is an eternal and undying truth, but a truth which is incomplete, in which not everything has been revealed. We are facing a new consciousness of the relationship between the saint and the genius, between redemption and creativeness.

The way of genius is another type of religious way, equal in value and equal in dignity with the way of the saint. The creativity of the genius is not "worldly" but truly "spiritual" activity.

> *The way of genius is another type of religious way, equal in value and equal in dignity with the way of the saint. The creativity of the genius is not "worldly" but truly "spiritual" activity.*

In every truly creative genius there has been the sainthood of the Creative Epoch, another kind of sainthood, more sacrificial than ascetic and canonic sainthood. Genius is another kind of sainthood, but it can be recognized and canonized only in the revelation of creativeness. Genius is the sainthood of daring rather than obedience.

The creative way of genius demands sacrifice—no less sacrifice than that demanded by the way of sainthood. On the way of the creative genius it is just as necessary to abjure "the world," to overcome "the world," as on the way of the saint.

But the way of creative genius demands still another sacrifice: the sacrifice of an assured position.... We who have entered on the creative way, the way of genius, must give up the quiet havens of life, must renounce the building of our own house, the safe and assured ordering of our personality. Only one is capable of this sacrifice who in it can transcend the bounds of "the world." The way of creative genius means casting off from all the safe coastlines. Genius is essentially tragic; it is not containable in "the world," and not accepted by "the world."

The creative genius never responds to the demands of "the world"—they never fulfill the world's orders; they do not come under any of the world's categories. In genius there is always something of the unsuccessful from the world's point of view—almost uselessness for the world.

In genius there is nothing specific—it is always a universal sense of things, a universal upsurge towards another kind of being. Genius is integral being, universal quality; genius is always the quality of a person—not only of an artist, a savant, a thinker or a social worker. Creativity is religious in nature, for it involves resistance to "this world" by the artist's whole spirit. It is a universal assumption of another world and a universal impulse towards it.

Genius is holy inadaptability to "this world." The life of a genius holds moments of ecstatic happiness, but it does not know peace and calm joy; it is always in tragic disharmony with the world around it.

Creativity and Asceticism: The Genius and the Saint

> ***Creativity is religious in nature, for it involves resistance to "this world" by the artist's whole spirit. It is a universal assumption of another world and a universal impulse towards it.***

Genius is radically different from talent—it has nothing in common with talent. Talent is a differentiated gift, specific, corresponding to the demands of various forms of culture. Talent is the quality of an artist, a savant, a social worker, but not the quality of a person. Genius is the union of a nature having the quality of genius with some specific talent. Thus, an artist who is a genius combines in herself this "genial" nature with artistic talent. The nature of talent is not organic, not ontological, but functional. The nature of talent is not universal.

The nature with genius in it may burn out without having brought into the world anything of value. Talent usually produces values and is suitably esteemed. Talent is moderate and measured. Genius is always measureless.

The nature of genius is always revolutionary. Talent acts in the midst of culture, with its "arts and sciences." Genius acts in ends and beginnings and knows no bounds whatever. Talent is obedience; genius is boldness and daring. Talent is of "this world," genius, of another. The cult of saintliness should be complemented by the cult of creativity, for the ecstasy of creativity is no less religious than the ecstasy of sainthood. Not saintliness alone, but genius also, is a way. The potentiality of genius, like the potentiality of holiness, lies in every image and likeness of God.

The will to genius is a courageous overcoming of "the world." Genius is a positive revelation of the image and likeness of God in us, a revelation of our creative nature, a nature which is "not of this world."

> *The nature of genius is always revolutionary. Talent acts in the midst of culture, with its "arts and sciences." Genius acts*

> *in ends and beginnings and knows no bounds whatever. Talent is obedience; genius is boldness and daring. Talent is of "this world," genius, of another.*

The gifts of God are endlessly varied, the ways of God are varied, and in the house of the Father there are many mansions. There were saints who had a special gift of the mystic contemplation of Divine mystery.... Other saints had the gift of beauty.

On the way of creative genius it is possible that a special new type of monasticism should arise. This way demands no less renunciation of "the world" and its goods than the way of monasticism as traditionally recognized. The life of genius is a monastic life in the world.

Only the religious way of creativeness carries mystic asceticism out to the real overcoming of this world, to the setting up of "another world."

CREATIVITY WILL SAVE THE WORLD

Nicholas Berdyaev
From "Creativity and Asceticism: The Genius and the Saint," *The Meaning of the Creative Act,* 1914, Chapter 7. Translation

Creativity and Culture

N.B. Excerpts from "Three Epochs: Creativity and Culture," The Meaning of the Creative Act, *1914, Chapter 14. Translation © 1955 by Donald A. Lowrie*

Topics: Three Epochs of revelation; the Absolute Man; symbolic v. realistic creativity; the complete transformation of life

The world is passing through three Epochs of Divine revelation: the revelation of the Law (the Father), the revelation of Redemption (the Son) and the revelation of Creativity [the Spirit]. It is not given to us to know the definite chronological limits of these three Epochs; they are all co-existent. Today, we have not fully lived out the Law, and Redemption from sin has not yet been completed, although the world is entering a new religious Epoch.

The three Epochs of Divine revelation in the world are three Epochs of the revelation about mankind. In the First

Epoch, our sin is brought to light and natural Divine force is revealed; in the Second Epoch, we are made sons and daughters of God and redemption from sin appears; in the Third Epoch, the divinity of our creative nature is finally revealed and Divine power becomes human power.

The revelation about mankind is the final Divine revelation about the Trinity. The final mystery is hidden in this, that the Divine mystery and the human mystery are one, that in God there is hidden the mystery of persons and in persons the mystery of God.

> *The revelation about mankind is the final Divine revelation about the Trinity. The final mystery is hidden in this, that the Divine mystery and the human mystery are one, that in God there is hidden the mystery of persons and in persons the mystery of God.*

God is born in us and we are born in God. The ultimate revelation of humanity means the revelation of God. Not only is God in us but we are the image of God; in us Divine development is realized. We are participants in the Divine Trinity.

We bear within ourselves a double image and likeness: that of the universe and that of God. The final revelation of humans is the final revelation of the universe and of God. The anthropological revelation, the revelation of persons in the Creative religious Epoch, is at once a cosmic and a Divine revelation. Through our creativeness, God in the world is finally revealed.

And in its religious depths the anthropological revelation is the revelation of Christ as Absolute Man. With the appearance of Christ in the world, our sonship with God, our likeness to God and our participation in the Divine nature are all revealed.

But Absolute Man is not complete and finally revealed in the appearing of Christ the Redeemer. The creative revelation of humanity is a continuing and completing revelation of Christ, the Absolute Man.

The anthropological revelation of the Creative Epoch is at once fully human and fully Divine. In it, we are deepened to the point of Divinity and Divinity is made visible to the point of humanity. The Divine-human nature of revelation is possible only in the creative act of the revelation of we, ourselves. The whole meaning of our Epoch is in the fact that it is passing over to the revelation of men and women.

> *The anthropological revelation of the Creative Epoch is at once fully human and fully Divine. In it, humanity is deepened to the point of Divinity and Divinity is made visible to the point of humanity.*

Hitherto, the world has known chiefly two ways: either the perfection of one's own soul or the creation of perfect culture. In creative experience, we will get away from the physical plane of the world and its laws. The whole fullness of our lives must become a creative act.

All the achievements of culture are symbolic rather than realistic. In culture, people have achieved not knowledge but symbols of knowledge; not beauty but symbols of beauty; symbols of love rather than love, itself; not the union of people but symbols of union; not power over nature but rather symbols of power. Culture is a religious failure—failure to achieve communion with God. It is only a symbolic expression of the final mysteries.

Culture is eternally and tragically unsatisfied. The crisis of culture is humanity's final will to pass over from symbolic and conditional attainments to the attainment of the real and Absolute. We have desired not symbols of truth, but truth, itself; not symbols of beauty, but beauty, itself; not symbols of love, but love, itself; not symbols of power, but power, itself; not symbols of communion with God, but that communion in very truth.

The creation of Eternity means bringing all culture to the very end, to the ultimate limit.... And we must admit that in the very nature of science, philosophy, morals, art, the state, economics, and even the visible church, there is latent a very evil endlessness, a poor kind of plurality.

The creativeness of the New Epoch will overcome culture from within rather than from without. The World-Creative Epoch can be only super-cultural rather than pre-cultural or extra-cultural; it accepts the positive religious meaning of culture, recognizes the great truth of every culture as over against all nihilism.

Culture is always opposed to anarchy or nihilism, to savagery or barbarism. The very failure of culture is a Holy failure, and through this failure lies the way to a higher being.

The world's culture must come to a new religious life, freely and immanently. Coming out of religious guardianship means entrance into religious maturity, the full expression of free religious life. There is a thirst for creativeness that will bring about a new life and a new world. The lover of truth desires nothing less than the complete transfiguration of life—the salvation of the world.

> *There is a thirst for creativeness that will bring about a new life and a new world. The lover of truth desires nothing less than the complete transfiguration of life——the salvation of the world.*

Nicholas Berdyaev
From "Three Epochs: Creativity and Culture," *The Meaning of the Creative Act,* 1914, Chapter 14. Translation © 1955 by Donald A. Lowrie

Creativity and the Church

N.B. Excerpts from "Three Epochs: Creativity and the Church," The Meaning of the Creative Act, *1914, Chapter 14. Translation © 1955 by Donald A. Lowrie.*

Topics: the church of Peter and the mystical Johannine Church; the heroic daring of creativeness

In the ultimate and secret depths of its being, creativity is of the Church. In creativeness, the Divine-human body of the world is created. And only in creativeness are the cosmology and anthropology of the Church finally and wholly revealed. In the historic Church, which corresponds to the early, infant stages of the development of new persons, there has not as yet been a revelation about humanity. A creative revelation is the only way to a rebirth and new development of the Church's waning life. Christianity has remained an unfinished revelation about our absolute significance and calling. The anthropological revelation of the Creative Epoch will be the finished revelation of God-manhood, the complete disclosure of Christ in the life of the world, of Christ uniting Himself with us.

> ***A creative revelation is the only way to a rebirth and new development of the Church's waning life.***

Christianity in history has fallen into the most terrible sin—sin against the Holy Spirit. Christianity has blasphemed against the Spirit whenever it has recognized the Church as finished, Christianity as complete, and creativeness as something forbidden and sinful. For life in the Spirit can be only eternally creative, and every stop or stay in the creative development of the Church is thus a sin against the Spirit. The life of the Church has ossified, has cooled, almost to the point of death, and it can be reborn only in our religious creativeness, only in the New World Epoch.

Christianity has grown old and wrinkled. It is a gaffer, two thousand years old. But the Eternal cannot grow old. And neither can the Eternal religion of Christ grow old. In the cosmos the redeeming sacrifice of Golgotha is consummated in all Eternity, and in all Eternity lives the mystical body of Christ. And the gates of Hell shall not prevail against this true Church of Christ.

> ***The life of the Church has ossified, has cooled, almost to the point of death, and it can be reborn only in our religious creativeness, only in the New World Epoch.***

It is only the temporal in Christianity which has grown old, it is only a certain Epoch of Christianity which has been outlived. The infant stage of the first education of mankind, the Epoch of guardianship and religious fear, has grown old and wrinkled, has lost its vivacity. The abnormality in Christianity is just this wrinkled old age of the infant. The immature and childish religious consciousness dug a deep abyss between God and the world, between the Creator and the creature.

But now we are turning to the spiritual body of the Church. The Christian renaissance of a new humanity, matured in the Spirit, moving out of the Epoch of fearfulness and guardianship, can take place only under the sign, not of the Church of Peter, but of John and the mystic Johannine tradition. This is the mystical and eternal Church of Christ, the visage of the Church, itself, revealing itself to us in ascent towards the heights rather than an adaptation to the lower depths of humanity. We have now matured into readiness for the new Church, not because we have become sinless and perfect, not because we have fulfilled all the commandments of the Church of Peter, but because our consciousness at the height of culture has attained mature and final acuteness, and our nature has been laid open to the point where its ultimate, first bases are revealed.

We have now matured into

> *readiness for the new Church, not because we have become sinless and perfect, not because we have fulfilled all the commandments of the Church of Peter, but because our consciousness at the height of culture has attained mature and final acuteness, and our nature has been laid open to the point where its ultimate, first bases are revealed.*

The historic Church of Peter is unable to satisfy the modern person; it is always answering questions which have not been asked; it soothes the wrong suffering, heals the wrong wounds; it has helped to save us from childish sins, but is powerless to help with the sins of maturity; it does not want to know anything new in us. The answer can be given only by the revelation of the mystery of the eternal, mystical Johannine Church of Christ. In this form, the Church opens to mature persons the boundless, measureless freedom of creativity in the Spirit. The secret will be revealed to us which has been concealed from infants in the period of tutelage—the secret that submission is not the ultimate in religious experience but only a temporary method; that in daring and sacrificial initiative this childish security must be overpassed, that sin will finally be conquered by heroic creativity. The security of historic, everyday churchliness must be sacrificed to the heroic daring of creativeness. Churchliness has hidden from us the heroic, sacrificial mountain way of Christ.

Nicholas Berdyaev
From "Three Epochs: Creativity and the Church," *The Meaning of the Creative Act,* 1914, Chapter 14. Translation © 1955 by Donald A. Lowrie

Christianity and the Creative Renaissance

N.B. Excerpts from "Three Epochs: Creativity and the Christian Renaissance," The Meaning of the Creative Act, *1914, Chapter 14. Translation © 1955 by Donald A. Lowrie.*

Topics: creativeness and eschatology; Christological self-revelation; creativity as religious duty

To overcome this religious servility is the first task of a Christian renaissance. We must know ourselves, not as the slave of God, but as free participants in the Divine process.

Christianity has not yet been fully revealed as a religion of love. Love is new, creative life—a life of grace in the Spirit. It can never be an object of education or morality. Love is not a law, and no one can be compelled to love.

With the Third, the Creative Epoch,

there is closely related a sense of the end, an eschatological perspective on life. In the Third Epoch, the Epoch of religious Creativeness, all ends and limits of the world's life and culture will be manifest. The creativeness of that Epoch will be directed essentially towards the final, rather than the penultimate; all its achievements must be not symbolic but realistic, not merely cultural but of the whole of life. The religious center of gravity will be transferred from the clerically-protective to the prophetically-creative.

But a prophetic religious experience cannot be an experience of passive expectation—this is an experience of active, creative striving, of great anthropological tension and effort. We cannot merely passively await the coming of Christ, we must be up and go toward Christ. The sense of the apocalyptic will lead to a new religious life only if it becomes actively creative instead of passively expectant. The coming of Christ, in which the Absolute Man will be fully revealed in all Christ's power and glory, is connected with our creative act, with an active anthropological revelation. Mankind's Christological nature will be revealed in our creative act.

The coming Christ will come only to a humanity which courageously accomplishes a Christological self-revelation, that is, reveals in its own nature Divine power and glory.

Christ will never come in power and glory to those who are not creatively active—they will never see the second face of Christ. God will eternally turn toward them the crucified, tortured and sacrificing face. To see the face of Christ in power and glory, we must reveal power and glory in ourselves by a creative act.

> *Christ will never come in power and glory to those who are not creatively active——they will never see the second face of Christ.*

The Epoch of Redemption, where only the crucified Christ is visible, will never end for those who do not perform the creative act which completely reveals human nature. They will ever remain in the Church of Golgotha, will never know the Church of the Coming Christ.

Defensive hostility toward religious creativeness is confirmation of an evil endlessness in redemption, itself; resistance to the completion and the fullness and the end of redemption. Religious opposition to the Third Creative Epoch desires a permanent endless redemption, resists the final solution of earthly life and the appearance of the Coming Christ, mighty and glorified.

The Church of Golgotha in which Christological truth is not completely revealed stands over against the Church of the integral Christ, where God is revealed completely. The coming of Christ and the full revelation of the whole truth about Absolute Man predicates that in creative activity we shall take our glorious and royal place in the world. To transform the Golgothan truth of redemption into a force hostile to creative revelation about mankind is a sin, a falling-away, which gives rise to world-religious reaction; it is hindering the all-resolving end of the world, the setting up of a New Heaven and a New Earth.

The sum of all the world's life and world's culture is the problem of creativeness, the problem of the anthropological revelation. All the threads come together at this point, everything comes to focus here. But we have not yet known true creativity in the final and ultimate religious sense of the word. Our philosophy is as yet only an introduction to the philosophy of creativeness rather than that philosophy, itself. And our present life is only a transition to creative life rather than creative life, itself.

> *The sum of all the world's life and world's culture is the problem of creativeness, the problem of the anthropological revelation. All the threads come together at this point, everything comes to focus here.*

What creativeness is is inexplicable. But our initiative towards a full realization of the creative life must be bold and our clearing of the way for it must be merciless. And we today, hesitating before our creative task and refusing creative initiative from a false sense of humility, cradled in passive obedience as the highest virtue, are not fulfilling our religious duty; we are not fulfilling the will of God.

Nicholas Berdyaev
From "Three Epochs: Creativity and Christian Renaissance," *The Meaning of the Creative Act*, 1914, Chapter 14.

Epilogue

N.B. Excerpts from Dream and Reality, Freedom and the Spirit, *and various articles*

Topics: anthropodicy; God-humanity; creativity and the self; the tragedy of creativity; Christian humanism; aesthetic contemplation as action

Many have written their justification of God, their "theodicy." But the time has come to write a justification of humans, an "anthropodicy." This book of mine is an essay on anthropodicy by means of creativeness.

God calls us to creative activity and to a creative answer to God's love. Every creative act strives towards the transcendent, towards passing beyond the borders of the given world. The creative act is always liberation and conquest. It is an experience of power. In essence, creativity is a way out, an exodus; it is victory.

> *God calls us to creative activity and to a creative answer to God's love. Every creative act strives towards the transcendent, towards passing beyond the borders of the given world.*

Creativeness must not be lowered in quality for the sake of a larger common ground and general acceptance, i.e. a greater conformity to the lower forms of communion—this is a sin against the Holy Ghost. Freedom from the reactions of "the world" and from opportunistic adaptations to it is a great achievement of the spirit. This is a way of great spiritual contemplation, spiritual collectedness and concentration.

> *Freedom from the reactions of "the world" and from opportunistic adaptations to it is a great achievement of the spirit. This is a way of great spiritual contemplation, spiritual collectedness and*

| *concentration.*

I confess a monopluralism, *i.e.* I accept both metaphysically and mystically not only the One, but a substantial plurality, the revelation in one God of a permanent cosmic plurality, a multitude of eternal individualities. The world-process is self-revelation of Divinity; it is taking place within Divinity. God is immanent in the world and in us. The world and we are immanent in God. Everything which happens with us happens with God.

The matter of creativity and of our creative vocation is not only a facet or one of the facets of my outlook, reached as a result of philosophical reasoning, but a source of my whole thinking and living—an initial inner experience and illumination.

Creativity stands in no need of justification from the religious or any other point of view: it is its own justification in virtue of our very existence; it is that which constitutes our relation and response to God.

It is imperative to bear in mind that our creativity is not a claim or a right on our part, but God's claim on and call to us. God awaits our creative act, which is the response to the creative act of God.

> ***God awaits our creative act, which is the response to the creative act of God.***

What is true of our freedom is true also of our creativity: for freedom, too, is God's summons to us and our duty towards God.

God does not reveal to us that which it is for us to reveal to God. In Holy Scripture we find no revelation concerning our creativity—not on account of its implied denial of human creativity, but because creativity is a matter for us to reveal. God is silent on this matter and expects us to speak. It is the concealed, rather than the revealed, will of God that we should dare and create, and such daring and creativity are a token of our fulfillment of the will of God.

Creativity for me is implied in the fundamental Christian truth of God-humanness, and its justification is the theandric (the union of Divine and human) theme of Christianity.

God's idea of the person is infinitely loftier than the traditional orthodox conceptions. The idea of God is the greatest human idea, and the idea of humans is the greatest Divine idea.

> *God's idea of the person is infinitely loftier than the traditional orthodox conceptions. The idea of God is the greatest human idea, and the idea of humans is the greatest Divine idea.*

We await the birth of God in ourselves, and God awaits the birth of us in Himself. The notion that God has need of us and of our response to God is admittedly an extraordinarily daring notion; yet in its absence, the Christian revelation of God-humanness loses all meaning.

The drama of God and His other one,

His human creatures, is present and operative in the very depths of Divine life. This is revealed not in theological doctrines but in spiritual experience, where the Divine drama passes into a human drama and that which is above is converted into that which is below. But this is in no way inconsistent with redemption: rather it is another moment on the same spiritual path and another act in the mystical drama of God and mankind.

Creativity, in my view, is not an "insertion" in the finite, not a mastery over the medium or the creative product, itself: rather it is a flight into the Infinite; not an activity which objectifies in the finite but one which transcends the finite towards the Infinite. The creative act signifies *ek-stasis*, a breaking through to Eternity.

> *Creativity is a flight into the Infinite; not an activity which objectifies in the finite but one which transcends the finite towards the Infinite. The creative act signifies* ek-stasis, *a breaking*

| *through to Eternity.*

I can remember how one summer day just before dawn I was suddenly seized by a tumultuous force which seemed to wrench me away from the oppressive spell of my despondent condition, and a light invaded my whole being. I knew then that this was the exalting call to creativity: henceforth I would create out of the freedom of my soul like the great Artificer whose image I bear.

What lay for me, as a Christian, in this experience was a realization of two processes, seemingly incompatible, but, by the paradox of life, really complementary—one redemptive, the other creative. I realized the fallacy of an exclusively soteriological religion. It is only in the creative act that we prevail over the oppression and enslavement of extraneous influences. The creative act reveals the absolute priority of the "self," the subject, over the "non-self," the object; but at the same time, it strikes at the root of the egocentric, for it is eminently a movement of self-transcendence, reaching out to that which is higher than oneself.

Creative experience is not characterized by absorption in one's own perfection or imperfection; it makes for the transfiguration of humanity and of the world; it foreshadows a New Heaven and a New Earth which are to be prepared at once by God and us. The ultimate fulfillment of redemption and the coming of God's Kingdom comprises a creative act on the part of each of us.

> *Creative experience is not characterized by absorption in one's own perfection or imperfection; it makes for the transfiguration of humanity and of the world; it foreshadows a New Heaven and a New Earth which are to be prepared at once by God and us.*

I have never failed to emphasize the religious, rather than the merely aesthetic or cultural, significance of creativity. My object has been not to justify creativity, but to show that, in its

Divine-human character, it is itself justification, inseparable from all the other acts which characterize God's relation to us and to the world.

Our creative act is doomed to fail within the conditions of this world. It is a tremendous effort which is destined never to succeed. Its initial impulse is to bring forth new life, to transfigure the world and usher in a New Heaven and a New Earth; but in the conditions of the fallen world the effort turns out to be unavailing; it comes up against the inertia, the laws and compulsions of the external world, pervaded as it is by the inexorable necessities. The attempt gives place to the production of aesthetic and cultural objects of a greater or lesser perfection. These objects, however, are symbols of reality rather than reality, itself: a book, a symphony, a picture, a poem or a social institution; but all these are evidence of the painful disparity between the creative impulse and its partial and fragmentary embodiment in the objective world.

I am far from denying the validity of culture and the value of its creative function in this world. We are committed by virtue of our destiny to the making of culture and civilization. And yet such making must not blind us to the fact that it is but a token of real transfiguration, which is the true, though unattainable, goal of creativity. "Realistic creativity," as distinct from "symbolic creativity," would, in fact, bring about the transfiguration and the end of this world, and the emergence of a New Heaven and a New Earth.

The creative act, alike in its power and impotence, is eschatological—a prefiguration of the end of the world.

> *The creative act, alike in its power and impotence, is eschatological——a prefiguration of the end of the world.*

The truth of Romanticism (which in other respects is an easy target for criticism) lies in its pervading sense of the insufficiency of all achievement within the finite, in its longing for and aspiration to the Infinite, or, to be more precise, to the Trans-finite.

The true aim of creativity, then, is the victory of "reality" over "symbol." To take symbols for reality is one of the chief temptations in life, and it has proved, on more than one occasion, the undoing of man and the betrayal of creativity.

Is it possible at all to pass from symbolic to realistic or transfiguring creativity? Or is this merely a dream which is destined to cause pain and torment to us but is never to come true? I, while impelled by a sense of the utter insufficiency of every creative realization, am looking for a creativity which aims at a real, not only a nominal and symbolic, transformation of this world.

My faith and hope, at first confident, elated and enthusiastic, is subsequently more temperate, difficult and painful.... But (I am not distracted) in the least from my belief in creativity; on the contrary, after the intense experience of ecstasy which I have described above, I never went back on my faith in our creative vocation. Ordinary workaday existence, with all its endeavors and exigencies, is interspersed with moments of true freedom and inspiration, and these alone infuse significance, authenticity and nobility into a world of unmeaning, make-believe and degradation.

> *I never went back on my faith in our creative vocation. Ordinary workaday existence, with all its endeavors and exigencies, is interspersed with moments of true freedom and inspiration, and these alone infuse significance, authenticity and nobility into a world of unmeaning, make-believe and degradation.*

I am a humanist, of course, since I believe in God-humanness and hence in the humanity of God. As a matter of fact, I believe that God is more human than we, or even that God is human, whereas we are inhuman. Belief in people involves and indeed is, belief in

God, and it cannot afford to indulge in illusions concerning ourselves.

> *I am a humanist, of course, since I believe in God-humanness and hence in the humanity of God. As a matter of fact, I believe that God is more human than we, or even that God is human, whereas we are inhuman. Belief in people involves and indeed is, belief in God, and it cannot afford to indulge in illusions concerning ourselves.*

The link between creativity and a pessimistic attitude towards life as it is given, with all its necessities, compulsions and conventions, made me attach a great importance to imagination, since without imagination there can be no creative activity. A creative act always rises above reality; it means imagining something other and better than the reality around us. The universe of discourse characteristic of religious orthodoxy is forced to deny creativity altogether, or at best only to tolerate it in a superficial way; because it (the discourse) is to a large extent the expression of an organized social collective, with its norms, taboos, prohibitions and conventions. The creative impulse, on the other hand, is absolutely unique, unbidden and lawless.

It is impossible to write a play, a novel or a lyrical poem without coming into conflict with the accepted norms and standards of moral and social behavior (unless one is satisfied with quasi-artistic pieces glorifying social, moral or religious puppets). Orthodox systems, whether social or religious, however, do not want to hear of these problems; their attitude to creative unrest, to the searchings and wrestlings of the spirit, is, quite consistently, one of suspicion and hostility.

I have already spoken of the unsystematic nature of my thinking. I have been much criticized for my carelessness and apparent incapacity for thoroughgoing philosophical analysis. I accept this criticism, since I am aware that the discursive and deductive processes of reasoning give place in my mind to sudden and disturbing visions. The thoughts to which I attach greatest importance came to me like flashes of lightning, like instantaneous illuminations.

When I begin to write I am sometimes carried away to the point of dizziness. My thought flows so fast that I hardly have time to write it down. Often I am forced to leave words unfinished so as to keep up with the rapid course of my thinking. I never think much about the form it takes: it seems to pour forth of its own accord, having, as it were, a word beyond or prior to the ordinary written or spoken words.

When I write I do not ordinarily read other books dealing with the subject with which I am concerned at the moment.... To do so would, so it seems to me, constrain the freedom of my thought and weaken my creative powers.

I write in response to an inner voice which commands me to transmit my mental experience. Writing is no luxury for me, but a means of survival, an almost physiological necessity. I write in order to testify to and free my mind from an overwhelming impression. In the white heat of creative ecstasy... none of the divisions and differentiations into subject and object (arise).

> ***Writing is no luxury for me, but a means of survival, an almost physiological necessity.***

Creative *works* are within time, with its objectifications, discords and divisions. But the creative *act* is beyond time: it is wholly within, subjective, prior to all objectification.

We ought to be able from time to time to fall back on contemplation in order to obtain relief from the activism of existence which, as we know too well today, can tear us to pieces. There is an intimate link between creativity and contemplation, although the current tendency is to oppose them.

Contemplation must not be understood as a state of sheer passivity or receptiveness: it comprises a distinctly active and creative element. The aesthetic contemplation of natural beauty is more than a state: it is an act, a breaking through to another world. Beauty is indeed that other world revealing itself in our own. And in contemplating beauty, we go out to meet its call.

> ***The aesthetic contemplation of natural beauty is more than a state: it is an act, a breaking through to another world. Beauty is indeed that other world revealing itself in our own. And in contemplating beauty, we go out to meet its call.***

Nicholas Berdyaev
Selections from *The Meaning of the Creative Act, Dream and Reality, Freedom and the Spirit* (all N.A.B.), and *Rebellious Prophet (Donald A. Lowrie)*

Invitation To Contemplation

The creative impulse is absolutely unique, unbidden and lawless.

Creativity is not passive reflection of the world. It is an active overcoming; a transfiguration of the world.

Creativity is a way out. An exodus. A victory.

Creativity infuses significance into a world of unmeaning, make-believe and degradation.

Creativity rises above reality. It imagines something other... something better.

Creativity does not believe that the world is really like that which is forced upon us.

The creative act is a breaking through to another world.

Creativity predicates freedom. It is the work of liberated women and men.

Creativity does not simply objectify the finite; it attempts to transcend the finite.

There is a tragic character of creativity as it is displayed in the products of culture and society. The tragedy lies in the painful disparity between the creative idea and its embodiment in the world.

The purpose of the creative impulse is the attainment of another life, another world, an ascent into being.

Art is a sympathetic living-into the world.

Creativity entails heroic resistance to every sort of thing that falls short of beauty and love.

All my life I have been a rebel. Mine is a revolt of the spirit and personality against the collective.

Creative *works* are within time, with its objectifications.... But creative *acts* are beyond time.

There is a Creator who produced created being, and within this created being creativity is possible. God awaits our creative act, which is the response to the creative act of God.

Creativity is not, like religion, a revelation of God—it is the revelation of humans, but of persons as participants in the Logos. God does not reveal to us that which it is for us to reveal to God.

In Holy Scripture we find no revelation concerning our creativity—not on account of its implied denial of human creativity, but because creativity is a matter for us to reveal. God is silent on this matter and expects us to speak. It is the concealed, rather than the revealed, will of God that we should dare and create, and such daring and creativity are a token of our fulfillment of the will of God.

The creative process is carried out in God from all Eternity. Creativity will continue creation; it will reveal the resemblance of our nature to the Creator. True creativeness is theurgy—activity together with God. God calls us to creative activity and to a creative answer to God's love.

Our stature and significance is in proportion to that in us which breaks through to Infinity. The power of art is its power to wrench out the roots of finitude and to turn our gaze to the Eternal.

Real artists have never been obedient to the given world.

Creativity never responds to the demands of the world, nor fulfills the world's orders.

Creative persons' intuition must remain at its high level, no matter how we may suffer from lack of communion with others and from their refusal to recognize the universal value of our creativeness. Creativeness must not be lowered in quality for the sake of a larger common ground and general acceptance... this is a sin against the Holy Ghost.

Real artists, true to their calling, have never been obedient to the given world. Creativeness must be free of any authority outside itself.

Freedom from the reactions of "the world" and from opportunistic adaptations to it is a great achievement of the spirit. This is a way of great spiritual contemplation, spiritual collectedness and concentration.

The artist is a free person, independent of the world, a person who refuses to adapt oneself. She cannot serve the nation or political parties, she cannot serve academic or professional aims. The artist cannot serve the good of mankind; he cannot be in service to anyone or any personal purposes.

The recognition of the absolute priority of freedom does not denote, as some would like to make out, individualistic self-assertion. Freedom of the spirit has in fact nothing in common with individualism: to be free is not to be insulated; it is not to shut oneself up, but, on the contrary, to break through in a creative act to the fullness of existence.

Belief in humans involves and indeed is, belief in God, and it cannot afford to indulge in illusions concerning humanity. My faith is an accusation of the age in which I live and a command to be human in this most inhuman of ages; to guard the image of persons, for it is the image of God.

Creativity stands in no need of justification from the religious or any other point of view: it is its own justification in virtue of the very existence of persons. It is that which constitutes our relation and response to God.

Creativeness must be free of any authority outside itself.

Life in God is freedom, untrammeled

flight; anarchy in the true sense of the word.

Creativity issues from freedom and is not subject to any laws whatsoever. Creativity demands free access to the living, immediate sources of being, and considers itself enslaved when this access to first sources is denied.

The final religious significance of creativity is immanently expressed in the free development of art.

In creativity there is an upsurge towards another being, another world, daring to approach the ultimate mystery.

The nature of creativity is always revolutionary. It is a universal assumption of another world and a universal impulse towards it.

Shall we begin?

For Additional Study

The Nicholas Berdyaev Resource Center [Tom Willett]
https://www.Nicholasberdyaevresourcecenter.org/

Berdyaev Discussion Group [Fr. Stephen J. Janos, Tom Willett, Софья Андросенко]
https://berdyaevdiscussiongroup.groups.io/

The Berdyaev Online Library and Index [Fr. Stephen J. Janos]
http://www.berdyaev.com

Nikolai Berdyaev [Dirk Kelder]
http://www.chebucto.ns.ca/Philosophy/Sui-Generis/Berdyaev/

Yakov Krotav's Berdyaev English Library [Yakov Krotav]
http://yakov.works/library/02_b/berdyaev/eng_00_berd.html

Berdyaev YouTube Channel
https://www.youtube.com/channel/UCh-CHku92_vaUmuXsTxS4xw

Contact
Tom Willett
creativity@willett.world

Acknowledgments

First, I must direct your attention to five towering figures in the preservation, translation and explication of the thought of Nicholas Berdyaev: Berdyaev's sister-in-law Evgenia Rapp, Father Stephen J. Janos, Dirk Kelder, Yakov Krotov and Donald A. Lowrie.

To Blaine Smith for inviting me to join the band. To Jim Hiskey for inviting me to join the family. To Brian McLaren for being the proof of concept. To Os Guinness for upping my mental game. To Jim Houston for raising the ante.

To Dan Beck for showing me the ropes. To Rich Gathro for showing me the way. To Warren Pettit for showing me the door. To Robin Crow for showing me the money.

To T Bone Burnett for teaching me to listen. To Sam Phillips for teaching me to see. To Tonio K. for teaching me to always be curious. To Mark Heard for teaching me how to be a friend. To Dr. Richard Halverson for teaching me to believe. To Eugene Peterson for teaching me to contemplate. To Thomas Merton for the Bourbon. To Stan Rosenberg for the Scotch. To Annie Dillard for teaching me to pay attention. To Simone Weil for teaching me to wait. To Henry Miller for teaching me that the way out is through. To James Thurber for teaching me to laugh. To H. L. Mencken for teaching me to complain. To Jim Thomas for teaching me how to hang my head out an open window in a speeding automobile and howl. To Kim Thomas for teaching me how to pray.

To Boris Badenov and Natasha Fatale for showing me how colorful Russians can be. To Lieutenant Yuri Rozanov for teaching me how to speak English with a Russian accent. To Colonel Rosa Klebb for teaching me how to get my kicks.

To Julie Atterbury Willett for love.

About the Editor

Tom Willett (1950-) is an American musician, entertainment industry executive, educator and author. Having toured and recorded extensively as a bass player during the '60s and '70s (Washington, D.C.), served as booking agent and manager for numerous artists in the '80s (Nashville), and worked as an Artist & Repertoire and Marketing executive in the '90s (Los Angeles and New York), Willett has been involved in the creation and marketing of more than 300 award-winning records. His work has been cited in "Billboard," "Rolling Stone," the "L.A. Times," "Entertainment Weekly," and *Image Journal,* and he has published dozens of articles encouraging creative excellence in music making and marketing.

As the co-founder of the Contemporary Music Center on Martha's Vineyard (the nation's only artists' colony for contemporary musicians) Willett helped train and develop more than 1,000 up-and-coming artists and music executives. Most recently he served as President of Dark Horse Institute in Franklin, TN.

Willett has written five books including *Van Gogh to Go,* a 3-volume series presenting the artist's most evocative quotes about art, work and spirituality paired with carefully-chosen paintings. With his father, the late Dr. F. Douglas Prillaman, Willett co-wrote *Stroke: The Road to Recovery* and *Understanding Stroke: A Guide to Medical Terminology.*

He currently entertains fantasies of a restless retirement in Montmartre on the Harpeth, Tennessee.

CREATIVITY WILL SAVE THE WORLD

Made in United States
North Haven, CT
01 November 2022